A Cup of My Coffee
Leadership Lessons from the Battlefield
to the Boardroom

Scott H. Dearduff

Scott H. Dearduff
CMSgt, USAF
Retired

DEDICATION

This book is dedicated to all of the great leaders I served with during 29 years in the United States Air Force. This includes leaders from all branches of the United States Armed Forces and several foreign countries.

CONTENTS

ACKNOWLEDGMENTS

The stories in this book are a combination of lessons I've learned over a long and challenging military career. There are so many people to thank for helping me learn and grow…they are too many to list here. For the actual production of this book, the following people deserve special recognition for their assistance; Robert Dearduff, Mags Dearduff, Amber Trout, Dr. Kenneth Woodcock, Suzette Cameron, Larry Jackson, Tom Dorl, Kevin Soltis, Kevin Slater, and many others for their preview and edit skills that contributed to the final product. I'd also like to thank the following for their special assistance in ways noted below:

- Robert D. Gaylor, Chief Master Sergeant of the Air Force #5, who is the reason the Mailbox story exists. It was his story, originally told at a graduation dinner which inspired me to adopt the theory into my own professional life. Chief Gaylor has inspired many over the years with his story telling abilities, and I am his biggest fan. I want to personally thank Chief Gaylor for concurring with the inclusion of the Mailbox story in my own words as part of this book. That lesson will help many over the years, and the Chief is the proud owner of it.

- Budreau Guidry, Chief Master Sergeant, USAF Retired. Chief Guidry is the reason for Chapter #6 and the title of this book. He was a hard-nosed leader who taught countless lessons to many of us who had the privilege of serving with him.

- Chas H. Browning, Senior Master Sergeant, USAF Retired. Sergeant Browning was highly influential in my early learning years and is the man behind Chapter #2, Stay in Your Lane. I learned many early lessons from him, and remain in awe of the example he set for those who followed.

- R. Wayne Purser, Colonel, USAF Retired. Colonel Purser is the only person I know well who has been awarded the Air Force Cross for combat heroics in Vietnam in 1975. He is the leader who taught me about knowing the Equipment Guy which is detailed in Chapter #3. Colonel Purser set a high bar for those of us who followed him when it came to knowing your people. I've never met anyone with as much talent in this area as him.

- Robin Rand, Lieutenant General, USAF. Lieutenant General Rand taught me many lessons in three years that we served together. More than what he taught me, I need to thank him for helping to bring clarity to many leadership situations we encountered along the way. His vision on leadership is admired by people around the world...none more than me.

- Gary L. North, General, USAF Retired. General North contributed the final pieces of my leadership development as we served during some very difficult times and at a very strategic level. Taking all of the lessons I had learned throughout my career, he was the one who helped me transition to strategic thinking. He taught me to see the impact we could have as leaders by simply being there for our people, trusting in their abilities, and holding them accountable for their actions.

INTRODUCTION

I strongly believe that leadership is an art, not a science. I've learned that leadership can be innate or it can be learned. However, I don't believe that anyone was truly born to be a great leader. Great leaders are formed over a long period of time through a series of opportunities and experiences. Without opportunities, even the greatest natural leader among us may never become known for great leadership.

History provides examples of superior leadership by men and women of great fame and fortune. However, we don't know that they were truly the greatest of their time or even their profession. Although I served alongside some great leaders in my time, I really don't know if they were the greatest of my era. What we do know, and that I concede, is that when leaders are presented with the opportunity to succeed or fail, they normally only get one chance. Those who get it right become known as great leaders, while those who fail are quickly forgotten--or remembered only for their failure.

There are few second chances when it comes to establishing your leadership legacy.

Great leaders devoted maximum effort to their growth and development. They studied other successful leaders, read books, attended universities, and grew personally by observing leaders in action. A melting pot of information, experience and wisdom that, when mixed together, created an ability within them to know what to do at the moment of truth, when real leadership was required for success or failure.

Great leaders are people of courage. Some have the courage to act in the absence of orders (direction). Some display leadership courage when difficult situations arise or when times are tough. And some make difficult and often unpopular decisions when it would have been much easier to make the popular decision…taking the easy way out.

A leader who acts courageously will be seen by his followers as strong and committed— they will want to follow. Leaders motivate their followers. Leaders conquer their enemies. Leaders inspire courageous acts.

Leadership is not a piece of paper or anything tangible, it's strictly an intangible art…but powerful nonetheless.

From the early days of my professional life there were examples of leadership around me every day. In trying to develop my own leadership skills and style I figured out that it would be impossible to be exactly like any one of the leaders I saw. Of the many leadership lessons I have learned in my lifetime, this may have been my first one:

Take away something from every leader you encounter!

There were also opportunities to view bad leaders in action, or to watch good leaders make mistakes. That led to the next lesson:

Learn from the mistakes of others and do not repeat them!

The lessons shared in this book are intended to help you grow and develop. Each lesson:

- is woven into a story that helps you remember the message
- has an easy to remember title to prompt your memory
- each story is true, and based on my personal experiences

I wrote this book in hopes that it will benefit you… or anyone who has aspirations to become a leader someday. I hope you will find this book helpful in your leadership journey. Good luck on your personal journey of leadership. So let's go out there and lead!

1

THE MAILBOX STORY

Back in my neighborhood there was one person who always got my attention. When I went past his home, I noticed several things right away. The grass in his yard was evenly cut and the edges of the yard were neatly trimmed. There were no leaves from the trees or loose trash laying on the yard. If his cars were in the driveway they were always clean and polished, appearing like they just came from the showroom floor. Even the windows on his house shined in the afternoon sun, never seeming to have any dirt or dust on them.

Being a curious young man, I decided one day that I would approach him and ask why these things were always as I had noticed. When I arrived at his yard and introduced myself; "Sir, can I ask you a question?" Without hesitation he replied, "Sure kid, go ahead."

I looked right at him with great curiosity and said, "Mister, why is your house and yard always kept so neat and your cars always so shiny?" He looked at me without much of an expression and simply said, "Because my name's on the mailbox."

After a few seconds of hesitation, trying to make sure I heard him correctly, I replied, "Sir, I'm not sure I understand." He looked at me again and smiled. Then he said; "Although we are neighbors, you don't really know me and before today we've hardly ever spoken. Even though we don't have a bond, you have formed an opinion of me based on what you saw when you went by. Each time you drive by my house you glance at the yard, the cars and even my house. Then as you continue to pass by, you look at the end of the driveway and you see my name on that mailbox indicating that my family lives here."

Still not sure what that meant or how it applied to my question I replied again. "Sir, I don't understand what your name being on the mailbox has to do with the things I noticed about your yard and your cars." He looked back at me and smiled again. Then he said; "You see, even though you don't know me you still form an opinion of me based on what you see. And I want your opinion of me to be a good one, not a poor one. Therefore I choose to make my house, yard, cars and all of my possessions look right in hopes that you will respect me because I take pride in the things that I have."

"Now I got it!" I said. Before walking away I thanked him. I had no idea how much this lesson on the neighborhood street would impact my life.

Years later I found myself working as a Command Chief Master Sergeant or senior manager in a large military organization. With thousands of people working in subordinate units, it would be hard to get to know each and every one of them. But it was essential that I set a good tone and have their respect during the few minutes of interaction that I would have with them.

I made it a point to show my personal pride in my uniform and everything that encompassed who I was. My uniforms were always pressed with sharp creases on the arms and legs. Boots/shoes always shined. Hair always properly groomed and never in need of a cut. It took a concentrated effort to make sure things were always in the right order.

On one particular day our base hosted some local government and business professionals for a tour. One of the popular stops was always to visit the ammunition storage area. Here we often showed the visitors how our Airmen built bombs that would go on the war planes in combat.

It was an exciting time for most civilians--normally a once in a lifetime experience. For me, this was routine and I looked for ways to make my time productive. It often became a chance for me to visit with some of the other Airmen who were not taking part in the demonstration…and there were always some standing off to the side as support, in hopes of meeting the dignitaries from the group, so they became my targets of opportunity.

On this day I walked down the line of Airmen who were standing in a military formation. I thanked each one of them for their patience and mostly for their dedicated service to the nation.

As I got near the end of the line a young Airman shook my hand and looked me in the eye. It appeared he wanted to talk to me about something but was unsure if he should. He said, "Chief, can I ask you a question?" "Sure kid, go ahead" I told him. He looked at me and said; "Chief, why do you always have shiny boots?"

As I glanced down it was easy to see why he asked, as they shined with great polish in the hot sun of this summer day in Arizona. Looking back at him I said; "That's easy young man, because my name is on the mailbox."

He looked at me with the same look I had back in the neighborhood. He asked; "What do you mean?" Pulling him off to the side of the formation I explained the mailbox story to him from my childhood. Then I said, "You know, you hardly know me as your command chief. You rarely get to see me out and around the organization because of the size and complexity of the place. And before today we've rarely spoken. But when you do get to see me you form an opinion of me based on what you see."

And then I pointed to the left pocket on my shirt and said, "And my name is right here on the mailbox." I could tell he was taking this lesson in easier than I did as a young kid in the neighborhood, so I did not belabor the point. Continuing on I said, "I want you to form a positive impression of me and not a poor one. I want you to trust me and follow me into battle."

Motioning to my boots I said, "By shining my boots, keeping my uniform clean and pressed, and my hair neatly groomed, you will remain confident that I take pride in what I do. These simple acts of showing pride in my possessions should translate into your trust in my ability to lead." With that he smiled and thanked me. Then he returned to the line and I pressed on. The lesson had been passed on.

Several months later we repeated the ammunition experience with another group of local dignitaries. Same drill, same line of Airmen. Same target of opportunity for me to engage with great American Airmen, so off I went.

As I worked my way down the line the second person encountered was that same young Airman from the previous visit. There, he stood tall, boots shining in the sun, uniform neatly pressed, and his shoulders drawn back. His chest stood out front, clearly indicating that he was a proud young man. We shook hands and smiled.

I pointed at his left shirt pocket and said, "Good to see your name on the mailbox." He smiled and said, "And good to see your name on your mailbox as well chief."

Reaching the end of the line, a supervisor from the section stopped me and said; "Chief, can you tell me that mailbox story?" I looked at him and said; "What story is that?" He smiled at me and said, "I don't know, but you told my Airman some story about a mailbox the last time you were here. And, ever since that day, he comes to work with his boots shined and his uniform is neatly pressed. His hair is always clean cut and he is neatly groomed." After a short hesitation he continued: "And his training records are always up to date and when he completes his work, he is the first one to volunteer for more, or he simply helps the others with their work. He seems to take great pride in everything he does!"

I smiled and looked at the supervisor. I said, "My friend, you just told me the mailbox story." Turning to walk away, I glanced over at the proud young man at the front of the line and realized that he not only ingrained the mailbox story into his own life, but he impacted others through his actions.

The Lesson

Put Your Name on the Mailbox by showing pride in yourself and all that you own or control

- *People will form an opinion based on what they see, even before they know you*

- *Employees will develop confidence in you as a leader and follow you into battle*

THOUGHTS FOR SUCCESS:

When you apply **the Mailbox Story** to yourself in all personal matters, you will directly impact the rest of the team in a positive way. You will begin to see tangible benefits in all the important things you do for your team and your company.

The benefit of this lesson is simple. Your employees will trust you and follow with greater passion. They will likely adopt this same theory for themselves, and implement pride in themselves. Overall, the organization or your team will be much better off. Goals will come easier when people take great pride in what they do.

Of course you can translate that into other areas and make it about more than just how you dress and appear. Everything you do as a leader is not that simple. There are going to be tough decisions to make, changes to implement, and downward directives from the boss that are not easy to accept. There may even be some tragic personal or business matters to deal with.

Tough missions will come easier through collaborative efforts of teams who all take pride in what they do. While it won't be easy, it can be done by incorporating this lesson into your leadership toolkit.

I believe this lesson can carry you through even the toughest of days. It certainly helped me through seven years of combat deployments. This lesson helped me remain prepared for many tough days, and many tragic events.

Remember that your name is on the mailbox when speaking to people, walking around their shop within the organization and even at company gatherings.

Some people say that you are in a glass bowl when you become a leader. Others call it by different names and take different approaches. I've always felt that as a leader or manager within my organization I assumed a higher level of responsibility for personal pride and accountability and therefore it was easy to put forth the extra effort required to set the right example.

Leadership is a tough art to master, but starting out by putting your name on the mailbox will certainly help you get on your way. So, shine those shoes, iron those clothes, and get out there and put *Your Name on the Mailbox*.

2

STAY IN YOUR LANE

The day was long and the action was intense. A battle had been fought, and although it was only against a simulated enemy, our forces had overcome many obstacles and emerged victorious. In the United States military we were often tested on our ability to accomplish the wartime mission through a series of official tests and inspections. Undoubtedly, this one was the toughest one we would face for many years.

During this particular battle my duty was to run the radio and telephone communications center that was responsible for the direction and control of all responding forces. At this time in my young career, I considered myself qualified beyond any of my peers and many of the superiors with whom I worked. The worst part was that I often let it be known through my words and actions without realizing how I was coming across.

With the results of the inspection posted it was clear that we had done well to defeat the enemy. There were even comments about the expertise of the unit's "command and control element", which I felt somewhat responsible for.

I was proud of my actions and took the praise with a great big smile. Everyone around me seemed pleased at my ability to handle this tough duty and they let it be known publicly. It was a great time for me and I could not have been more proud.

Little did I know that I was showing it far too much publicly and actually started getting out in front of myself. Although it was good to have the confidence, I soon learned that I was crossing the line and had become cocky. In the military as in the private sector, there is a fine line between being confident and being cocky. It seemed I had reached new levels of cockiness.

A few days after the inspection was over I was visited on my post by the manager of our team who had almost twenty years of service under his belt at the time. He sat with me quietly, watching me control the actions of the on duty forces.

His actions led me to believe that he was not even paying me any attention and that I was in complete control. His duty was to manage the entire operation and his reputation was sound. Some of his predecessors led differently, often giving me free rein to run more than my share, and often times they sat back and let me run theirs. As the day progressed, he watched with more intensity and then finally spoke up.

The conversation began when he started by saying; "So you think you are pretty good at this controller business don't you?" I said; "Yes I do, and I proved it during the last inspection." Smiling back at me he said; "You think you have this all figured out don't you?" And again I replied; "Yes I do, and everyone seems to agree with me." He continued his line of questioning me by asking; "You think you are smart enough to do my job don't you?"

Even though I was 17 years his junior and operated at four enlisted pay grades below him, I said; "Yes, I think I can." In his own quiet, yet stern way, he looked at me and continued the conversation: "Well you are not." Momentarily stunned, I wanted to ask him what he meant by his comment, but before I could ask he said; "You're not as smart as me and you cannot do my job.

There are just so many things you don't know at this point in your career and with your limited experiences. In fact, you are not even the best controller we have in this unit. Nor are you the best senior technician we have on this team."

I could feel anger overtaking my emotions. My manager was telling me that I was not good enough to be considered the best at what I was assigned to do. This was a tough thing to hear and I wanted to argue and defend my actions, but he continued; "When you decide to concentrate your efforts on the duty assignment I have given you and stop worrying about doing my job or others jobs, you will begin the process of becoming the best controller we have. And when you stop trying to act like a manager and perform the duties and responsibilities assigned to you as a senior technician, then and only then will you have a chance to become the best at those two things."

He hesitated for a moment while I soaked in what he had said. All the while I was thinking about all the praise I had received from the inspection results and wondered why he would feel this way.

Before I could even ask a question he went on in his calm tone; "When you learn to concentrate on being who you are and what you are, and fully learn the art of Staying in Your Lane, you will likely become a real expert and be recognized as such. On that day I will walk in here and promote you to the next rank."

For a moment I was excited about what I was hearing as it seemed there was hope for me when only a minute before it sounded like I was going nowhere fast. He went on; "And once you learn to become an expert at that level, and handle the duties you are assigned, then I will walk in and promote you to the next rank again."

His message seemed to say that I had reached outside of where I was supposed to be and was trying to operate at a level beyond my years. A lump had formed in my throat and I was angry at hearing this direct and potentially negative feedback.

The devastation of that conversation stuck with me for days. I spoke to nobody about it, and just tried to digest it for what the message seemed to be. Was he really telling me that I was not good at what I was doing or was there another message? I thought long and hard about each and every word that he shared with me and determined that this could be a very positive learning moment for me. My actions in handling this feedback would need to translate into a positive change in behavior.

His message was clear; **stay in my lane** and continue to operate there to the best of my ability. He was telling me to become good at what I was before trying to move on and be whatever was next. There it was right in front of me, a very clear lesson in leadership and it was given to me absolutely free. It was not learned in a classroom, nor from a textbook, just straight forward from a man who was an expert with years of experience.

The Lesson

***Stay in Your Lane* by concentrating all of your effort and energy on the mission or task that you have been assigned**

- *Don't focus any energy or effort on where you might be assigned next*

- *Spend all of your time on the position that you currently hold*

THOUGHTS FOR SUCCESS:

A week after the discussion my energy was fine tuned and focused on just what he had said. Every effort was made to learn every aspect of the duties assigned to being a controller. I even found a promotion guide that was provided to each individual and began to study the roles and responsibilities expected of each level.

I figured the only way I could become an expert was to know what the expectations were, and then learn them so well that each one would become routine in my daily actions.

Within a few months my confidence was rebuilt in performing the tasks I was asked to accomplish. Rather than talk about what I did, my actions spoke for themselves. Those around me started to notice that I was gaining deeper knowledge of the controller position and my actions were appreciated. As a senior technician, my actions became clearly focused on what I could do for others rather than what I could do for myself.

Six months after that discussion about staying in my lane a surprise came by way of a phone call. The manager who taught me this lesson had moved on to another assignment, or he would have made the call himself. The caller simply said, "Hey, congratulations, you've just been promoted." Immediately my thoughts went back to that day when I learned this ever so important lesson and there was nothing I could do but smile. His theory was right-on and the lesson had stuck.

First I had to get back in my lane. Then once I was actually there, I had to learn to stay in my lane. The path to success became clear when I learned to stay in my lane.

Throughout the next 15 years this lesson played a valuable role in my development and success. Often when others were concentrating on the next promotion or the next duty position, I found myself locked in my lane and concentrating on being the best at whatever I was assigned.

Soon the promotions came and before I could truly realize what had happened, my final promotion in the military was realized. During the last 9 years of my military career the opportunities to serve and lead were vast and the assignments varied. While my peers talked of what the next job was, I continued staying locked into my lane and demonstrated that I was an expert at being what I was.

I worked hard to master every aspect of the career field I worked in and operated well within my comfort zone on things that I began to enjoy doing. Although I was at the top of the rank chart and had many new responsibilities, I made sure that I never lost touch with what got me to this point, and never forgot where I came from. My lane was secure and my actions showed it without any explanation.

The transition from the military to the private sector was filled with daily challenges. Staying in my lane proved helpful in getting hired and eventually in setting a course for success.

On day one with a private sector company, a fellow employee who had a similar military career came to me with this advice. He said, "Come into the company and learn what it is they want you to do in your role. Don't get wrapped up in what others are doing, and don't jump in with answers when you hear them struggling with problems that you know how to solve."

I listened carefully, wanting to know if he had more. He said, "If you start getting into other people's business lanes without their permission, you will not succeed in the private sector." I looked at my colleague and said, "Are you telling me to stay in my lane?" He smiled and said, "That's perfect. Stay in your lane and you'll do just fine."

Speaking out on issues that are not in my lane in the private sector could bring instant doubt about my intentions. I've found the best option is to keep my opinions close at hand until they are asked for. When asked for my opinion, I'm ready and happy to share my thoughts. Colleagues in the private sector accept these thoughts with openness and respect. They have often commented on the value of my leadership experience, and how much they appreciate my inputs at the right time and place.

While this has worked for a military leader transitioning to the private sector, it will also work for a manager moving into a new line of business or from one company to another. Clearly, moving into a new role and stepping out of your lane could be a real troubling situation...Stay in your lane!

So there you have it, a leadership lesson that is so simple, yet quite important. A lesson that helped me gain the additional focus needed to ensure success. This lesson helped bridge many challenges over the years.

Now I find it works in the private sector and can even be used in your personal endeavors. Here's the bottom line; concentrate your efforts on the assignment you have and never worry about being something you are not or may never become.

It's as simple as this, just *Stay in Your Lane!*

3

THE EQUIPMENT GUY

Walking through the hallway one cold afternoon my commanding officer was sharing his thoughts on an upcoming mission for our unit. We came across a young Airman in the hallway and the colonel stopped and engaged him, something that he always did. After a few short minutes of conversation, we moved on and continued the discussion.

We had just encountered one of more than 386 people in our unit. I thought to myself there was no way that he knew everyone in the squadron or could remember their names. But during that brief encounter, the colonel spoke with that individual like they had known each other for years. I barely recognized the young man as a member of the unit and would have walked right past him in the local town if we were both out shopping in civilian clothes. But the colonel knew him by name and after a short greeting, asked the young man how his puppy dog was doing. I stood there in shock at what I saw.

How did the colonel know that this young man even had a puppy…or that it was sick? This level of knowledge about one of the Airmen was hard to grasp. Here was a man with huge responsibility for national security, but he knew the names of the masses who worked for him. I wanted to know more.

As we moved into his office to continue the talk, I stopped him and asked, "Sir, how is it that you knew that young man and how did you know he had a sick puppy dog?" He smiled his country smile and said, "Scotty, I make it my business to know them."

That seemed simple enough to me, but I was still confused. "What does that mean exactly?" I said. He looked at me again and said, "Each member of the unit is important to the mission. They all have a part they play, a role they fill. If I don't know them, how can I know what they do, or if they are doing it well?" It seemed to make sense to me now. And we moved on.

Over many years and much travel the lesson became a part of my personal philosophy. Traveling the battle fields of Iraq and Afghanistan, I would speak to large groups of Soldiers, Sailors, Airmen and Marines. Using this lesson I was able to motivate many thousands by helping them understand that each and every one of them was important to the mission and how each played a significant part.

My address to the audiences went like this:

Who remembers the Super Bowl in 2008? The game was between the New York Giants and the New England Patriots that ended on a Giants touchdown, but only after the most amazing catch ever in a big game.

With just minutes to go and the Giants trailing the Patriots, the Giants quarterback found himself scrambling for his life, and the life of the Giants if they were to win the game. He ducked, dodged, and finally ran his way free before launching a pass more than 40 yards down field to a heavily guarded receiver.

Miraculously, the receiver jumped between two defenders and grabbed the ball out of thin air with one hand, pinning the ball on the top of his helmet while falling sharply to the ground. He held on to that ball, creating a first down and a huge momentum swing for the Giants. They went on to score and eventually win the

Super Bowl against the heavily favored Patriots.

There were many heroes that day for the Giants who were all celebrated on national television. As I watched the celebration I wondered who the most important person on the Giants team was that day. Who was the person who contributed significantly to the victory?

What do you all think? Who was the most important person on the Giants? (The most common responses were always like this): "It's the quarterback who threw the pass." "The receiver who caught that pass." "The coach, the offensive line, the entire team!"

Once I had all of their answers, I would continue:

Some of you think the quarterback, the receiver or even the coach was the most important person on the Giants. But I think you have all overlooked one person whose performance for the team is crucial to every player on every play, and every aspect of the game. He has the most direct impact on individual performance or lack thereof. He makes sure everything is right even before the first whistle. Long before the players arrive and the training staff begins taping up ankles this guy is already on the scene setting up the gear. He makes sure the quarterback has the right length of cleat on his shoes to provide the best grip of the field. He even makes sure the footballs have the right amount of air so the kicker can perform at the crucial moment.

Yes, I'm talking about **the equipment guy.** He is the one who stands steady on the sideline waiting for a player to come out of the game with an equipment malfunction. Quickly assessing things, he gets the player back on the field. He performs on short notice and with exacting perfection. He finds ways to patch things up that are not replaceable.

And when it's all said and done, the quarterback is standing on the podium announcing that he is going to some fantastic theme park to celebrate with his family, the equipment guy is already busy putting things away, and making sure they are ready for the next game.

The equipment guy hardly gets to celebrate the victory, he just goes back to work. The equipment guy is hardly thanked for his contribution, but he works harder than anyone on the team. The equipment guy may be the least athletic of the entire staff, but yet he has the greatest impact.

And nobody knows his name.

The Lesson

Spend time getting to know the Equipment Guy on your team or in your organization and ensure he knows how valuable he is to the team's success

- *Each and every equipment guy (people on your team) will feel more important because you show that you value their contribution*

THOUGHTS FOR SUCCESS:

Do you know the equipment guy in your organization? Is there someone who works behind the scenes, making sure that everything happens? Is that person quiet and unassuming, asking little for the work he does and never expects public recognition. Does that person give maximum effort for the team and its leaders?

If you know the equipment guy you will have proven that you are in tune with the entire team. The equipment guy will work hard for you and will ask for little. The equipment guy will be there when you need him, probably without asking, and he will be ready to provide the necessary help. I say you have to know the equipment guy and his puppy dog as the colonel taught me many years ago...just make it your business.

The lesson that I learned that day had a huge impact on me then and on many days long into the future. I apply it even today in my journey through the corporate world because it's a valuable lesson.

As your leadership responsibility grows, you will have to set aside time and find ways to get to know the equipment guy. Often times I sat face to face with those equipment guys on my teams and used a simple phrase to help break the ice.

Introducing myself with a firm handshake and looking directly into their eyes I would simply say, "Tell me your story." Some of the looks were priceless. There were countless responses like, "I don't have a story." An easy response to that was always; "Yes you do, everyone has a story."

Normally after some coaxing, they would come up with some interesting things about themselves or their lives. You could learn more about a person in 5 minutes than most people can after months or years of working together.

Even the shy people would eventually open up. Telling their story was a comfort zone for most, and once they got rolling sometimes it was hard to get them to stop. After a period of rambling you might have to stop them and say "OK, you've told me a lot so far, let me see if I can remember all this." By the end of the short encounter you will know things about them and can lock that data away for future use. They will appreciate that you took the time to remember.

Go get to know **the Equipment Guy** and don't forget to *make him or her your business*!

Ed Wagner Jr.

Who is he you ask?

The Equipment Guy, NY Giants since 1977

4

JUST FIX TRUCKS

The heat of the Kuwaiti desert was nearly unbearable during the summer months. Operating in heat that exceeded 120 degrees made even the easy tasks of completing a mission difficult. But for those who were assigned there during their deployments, there were only two choices: complete the mission in that awful heat, or fail. For American service members, the second choice is not an option.

During one particularly hot September day in that Kuwaiti desert the travel itinerary included a visit to the transportation unit that held responsibility for all motor vehicles on the compound, around the clock, seven days a week.

This group consisted of vehicle operators, mechanics, supervisors and managers. They awaited my arrival and were all standing in formation as I entered the building. Quickly realizing that this formation was too formal and would hinder my ability to talk with the group and get the message across, I told the senior staff person to have them "fall out" of formation and gather around me.

It was hot, the building had no flow of air moving about, and the distinct smell of vehicle fluids filled the air.

Once the crowd of 40 or so got themselves situated in close proximity, I began talking about the things that were going on around the battlefields of Iraq and Afghanistan. It was always my intent to share the "big picture" of the combat zone, as each group was confined to their own battlespace and their particular mission.

Once that discussion was complete and their questions were answered, we paused to honor those who had given the last full measure on the fields of battle. It was another way of keeping them attached to the front lines as they completed their mission behind the front lines in relatively safe areas.

Next it was time to discuss my point of the trip. To ensure that each of them knew the mission and how they fit in. I looked around the group and found a young face in the crowd, one who tried to avoid eye contact with me in fear of being called upon for some question or discussion. I walked directly over to this one particular young man and asked his name.

Once he shared his name and his home town I asked him a simple question. It went like this; "So, what is it that you do for the mission?" He looked at me shyly and said; "I just fix trucks."

I snapped back quickly and asked; "Is that important to the overall mission?" After hesitating for several seconds, he said; "I think so." "What do you mean, I think so?"

He tried again by saying; "I think it is…and without hesitation he went on…You see that truck over there, that's the one I am working on. Once I get it fixed it will go back out on the flight line and will be used by the aircraft maintenance team to carry a tire for one of the refueling aircraft. If they cannot change that tire before it's supposed to fly tonight, the plane may not complete its mission."

I asked him for more information on this train of thought he was sharing. I said; "So what if that one plane does not complete its mission tonight?" Looking me directly in the eye, he said, "If that refueling plane does not fly tonight and have gas available for the fighter jets to keep flying, one of them may not be able to get their bombs on target in time."

Now we were getting somewhere, so I asked; "And what if they don't get their bombs on target, so what?" His confidence was now building with each response. He said; "If they don't get bombs on target in time, some Soldier, Sailor, Airman or Marine on the battlefield may die because they were not protected."

BINGO! He nailed it and his words could not have been better scripted. This young man had no idea that I would call on him, no idea what I might ask even if I did. But when he was put on the spot and asked if his job was important or not, he knew and explained it with conviction. His ability to relate "I just fix trucks" to bombs on target was the best answer I had ever received to that question.

The Lesson

Make each employee understand how their task is important to the overall mission, even if they just fix trucks

- *They will feel good about their contribution and become highly productive*

THOUGHTS FOR SUCCESS:

Knowing the mission of your team or organization is extremely important for the success of the business. Knowing how you fit into that mission is even more vital. Most of us can recite a mission statement, remember the key words and phrases, and even explain it to outsiders. But the real secret is to be able to articulate how each of us fits into the mission and how important our role is.

Imagine if everyone in that unit had the same level of understanding that he had. Imagine if they all felt that way about their contribution. That unit would never fail to have the trucks ready for the mission.

There's no doubt that the aircraft he referred to completed its mission, the results are in the statistics on the battlefield. The mission was highly successful because of a young man in a back shop for vehicle maintenance who knew how important his part was in mission accomplishment.

Not every organization I have worked for has had this level of understanding across the ranks. Some organizations have failed to explain the mission to its team and left people to believe that they were just there to work, and that their work was insignificant.

Those organizations did not have records of success and I am glad that I was not deployed with them into combat where the stakes are extremely high.

Do you work in an organization that fails to explain the mission to its people? Do employees just come to work, complete tasks, clock out and go home? If so, and if you are in charge, you might consider changing this one thing today and watch the impact it has on the overall picture.

If you are responsible for five or fifty people, you should take the time to explain their part to them, making sure they understand and can articulate how and why they matter.

This same theory works in the civilian world just like it does in combat units. An executive in a large company told this story to illustrate the same point during a conference that I attended with business leaders from the banking, insurance and financial planning industries.

He shared that during a lunch meeting with some colleagues at a local restaurant they noticed a young bus boy who was working diligently to clear the tables around them, making sure that each one was ready for the next customer in minimal time.

They called him over to their table and asked, "Why are you working so hard on clearing those tables?" He looked at them and said, "We have a mission of increasing our revenue by 8% this year." One of his colleagues asked, "So what does that have to do with a bus boy clearing tables?"

The young man stopped and said to the men at the table, "You see, between 11am and 1pm is our busiest time for the lunch crowd. If I can keep the tables clean and ready in minimal time, more customers can come in and enjoy the food, thereby increasing the overall revenue for the business." Each of the men sat in stunned silence as they realized they had just learned a valuable lesson about business from a minimum wage earning bus boy.

When people feel connected to the mission, they will work harder for you and produce better results for your business. They will invest themselves in the business to see it succeed. Isn't that what every business owner wants anyway?

For those who fail to accomplish this leadership task, the results can lead to failure. It could be failure of the people to feel important. Or it could lead to failure of the people to invest in the effort. It may even lead to failure for the company. Get engaged with workers at all levels and make sure they know the mission of the company. Spend time with them to ensure they know how important they are and how their effort plays a critical role in the overall mission.

Remember, even the guy whose mission is to j*ust fix trucks* has an important role, and he can significantly help you and your business succeed.

5

WALK THE MILE

For twenty-two years my work mainly consisted of Security and Law Enforcement Operations with little exposure to other career paths or lines of business. Because of the extensive time I spent with nuclear security operations and presidential security, some considered me a real expert in those fields.

But with professional advancement came opportunities to manage and lead people who had different professional backgrounds and cared little about what my past consisted of. All they wanted to know was what I could do for them now that I had taken over a position at the Executive Director level. In order to gain their confidence and build credibility, I had to act fast and show them I was serious.

My new role included responsibility for aircraft maintenance, an area that was unfamiliar to me. There were hundreds of young men and women who spent their days and nights working hard in very harsh conditions to keep the fleet of military fighter aircraft operational to meet the demands of the mission. It was obvious to everyone that my background lacked any maintenance experience, there was no disguising that.

In the early days of this two year tour of duty, one of the units offered to host me to "launch a jet" with them so that I could better understand what they did out on the flight line— the front line. I told them I would be honored and just needed to know what day and time.

They initially told me that I could launch a jet on Tuesday at 1015 and that I should arrive at 0945. I looked at them with a puzzled gaze, I said, "I thought you told me this was a tough part of the operation?" They looked back just as puzzled and said that it's not only tough, it's one of the most critical operations that we do.

So I said, "Then it must take longer than 30 minutes for this to happen. I'm curious what time does the young man I will be working with arrive?" Eventually they said, "Well he shows at 0615 to get his tools, stand in a pre-mission briefing, and conduct a pre-walk of the area for foreign objects that may hinder the jet engine during the operation...but you don't have to worry about any of that, just show up at 0945." I looked back and said, "I will see you at 0615."

Arriving at 0615 in the morning it was already 95 degrees outside and somehow it's warmer on the flight line. Upon arrival there was a strong young man standing at the door waiting to greet me. He introduced himself and said that we could get started right away, not wasting any time in case I had questions. Off to the tool barn we went.

After we both took turns dragging the 100 pound tool box out to the aircraft parking spot, we headed for the briefing room. My questions came like the rounds out of the 20 millimeter guns on the aircraft and he handled them with ease. As we reached the briefing room the others were standing tall waiting for us.

We joined the formation and listened intently for assignments, safety messages and any other additional notes from the boss. When he was done, the boss said "We have a special guest with us today…" But before he could say anything, I motioned to him and cut him off. Then I simply said, "I'm just another worker standing in formation, waiting to go launch my jet, walking a mile in your shoes."

The rest of the experience was fantastic and I likely learned a ton more than I ever imagined I could through the sweltering heat of the day and the pounding noise of the jets all around. I learned more about the person who was paired with me, the jet we launched, the team he was assigned to, and so much more.

Most important, I learned what it was really like to be out on the flight line at 95 degrees during early morning hours, looking for little rocks and pieces of metal that could damage a jet engine to the tune of about 100,000 dollars.

And I earned the respect of more than 200 people working on that team who undoubtedly passed that on to hundreds of others in the sister units. They commented that it was inspiring to have a senior leader walking the mile with them on the front lines, and it showed in their performance.

Throughout the next two years of that assignment, those same people lit up when I walked into a room. They showed new levels of motivation and talked about that jet launch as if it had just happened the day before, even some 24 months later.

Walking that mile in their shoes showed respect to the front line workers. And it helped me earn respect from those front line workers who handled this critical mission task each and every day. Walking that mile positively impacted my ability to lead in that organization where I had no practical experience.

Walking that mile contributed to a high degree of success from the Airmen I encountered that day which translated into a high degree of success for their unit.

The Lesson

Earn the respect and trust of your subordinates by Walking a Mile in their shoes, experiencing what they go through each and every day

- *Walk the whole mile and do it at random times with no fanfare*

- *Consider dressing like them while you are out there*
    - *If they wear specialty gear and a uniform, wear their gear and uniform*

THOUGHTS FOR SUCCESS:

Let's say you just got promoted to a new division of your company, one in which you have no practical experience. You were brought in to bring leadership and big picture expertise, maybe even additional business savvy to this area of the company. You are going to be given a certain amount of loyalty because of the position that you hold that is inherent in the title.

They will call you sir/ma'am, attend your meetings, and attempt to meet your requirements for completing projects. But for them to truly buy in, get on board with you, give their loyalty to you, and even come to the point of fully respecting you, they will need to see you out there "rolling up your sleeves" or digging in with them.

Yes, they understand that you have a job to do and that includes meetings, conference calls and many other agenda items that they may not ever need to understand. But if they think that you don't care enough about them to spend a fair amount of time walking in their shoes, then they will only work as hard as they feel obligated.

Don't fool yourself and think you can walk around and pass out ice cream on Friday and think that it meets the intent of this lesson. No, you have to walk the whole, undistracted, uninterrupted, mile. I used this philosophy at each assignment and with as many different teams as I could fit into my schedule. Walking miles in combat units came with additional commitment due to the extreme danger of those duties. Walking those miles gave me the most gratification because of the confidence that grew between us during those times.

This may be a simple lesson in humility for some, and yet for others it will be a real comfort zone. Simply put, you need to get out from behind your desk and walk a mile with someone in your organization. Things were different back in your day…times and equipment have changed. It will pay big dividends with your team if you get involved at their level.

That level of respect, on top of the loyalty they give you based on your position, will increase your ability to lead and accomplish the goals of the organization. Hey, you may even have fun like I did on that day out on the flight line. Have fun…get out there and **Walk the Mile**!

6

A CUP OF MY COFFEE

Placed in charge of a major project to provide professional education and development to a large group of employees, I began sending emails to request assistance from subject matter experts.

Times had changed and email was the newest tool we had for communications. We started to operate more on the email systems than any other communications medium, including telephones. Within days of sending the initial request, responses were coming in and people were committing to support the program that was being proposed. Most of the key players were on board…everyone seemed willing to help.

But there was one man who seemed to be holding out and not responding to my email requests. He was a true expert in areas of this project that would lend a high degree of credibility to the team…we desperately needed his presence. Without him, the project could fall short of the objective.

A second email was sent with no response. Then a third email, same thing, no response.

Finally after another week and a fourth email, a short response came through. It simply said, "Call my office." Picking up the phone immediately I spoke with a very polite secretary. She said, "He would like to see you on Monday at 1000."

It seemed strange to me that he wanted to meet in person; all I wanted was to get a commitment from him. It seemed there was little choice but to accept the meeting since we really needed him on this project. My hope was that he would have committed through email to supporting the effort.

He clearly saw me walk into the secretary's area from his office when I arrived 10 minutes early, but he did not call me in. At exactly 1000 he walked out, welcomed me, shook my hand with a firm grip and said, come and have *a cup of my coffee*.

He didn't ask if I wanted coffee, or if I even liked the stuff. But he brought me into the office and sat me down with a fresh cup of coffee. After a few minutes of personal chat about how I was doing and several drinks from the coffee mug on his desk, he said, "Now tell me what it is that you need from me for this project."

I said "All the details were contained in the email and that I just needed to know if you are on board for the project?" He looked at me and said, "Go ahead and tell me what it is you want from me."

I explained the details of the project, assuming that he did not understand the email. When I finished, he asked a few questions about the timing and the location for the project. Seeming satisfied, he said; "Good, now that is what I wanted to know about the project and I will be happy to assist."

With that he looked me right in the eye and said, "But, the

next time that you want something from me, you will show me simple respect by coming here and sitting down with me over a cup of my coffee. Then, and only then, after you show me some level of respect and common courtesy, you can explain what you need from me."

The look on my face must have been priceless. I still did not get the point and must have appeared confused. My confusion did not matter, because he seemed happy—and the most important piece of this endeavor was to gain his support.

Walking out of his office the message was still not that clear to me. I thought taking advantage of the technology seemed like the smartest way to go. He was trying to help me understand the value in seeing someone face to face rather than communicating strictly through electronic means. The true meaning of this lesson would not become clear to me until years later.

The Lesson

Meet people face to face over a cup of coffee to find out what you can do for each other and how you can collaborate for success

- *This face to face approach allows you to show respect to those you are dealing with*

- *Face to face efforts help gain commitment for your effort*

- *Don't rely on technology so much that you lose the ability to see people face to face*

THOUGHTS FOR SUCCESS:

There was no way to know the impact this leadership lesson would have on my success as responsibilities grew in scope. Over the next 15 years I found myself in situations where communicating messages to the people on my teams became critical to our success.

When there was actual geographic distance between us, the first step was always to pick up the phone and speak to them. After that initial discussion was complete, information could be sent via the email system to give them more details, support materials or to establish deadlines.

But the important part was giving them the respect of talking with them first. Of course the best plan would always be to see them face-to-face whenever possible when geography did not limit that ability.

The theory of face-to-face meetings proved to be the most effective way to gain support from others. Finding the right person for the part became much easier using this method. It even seemed as though it became hard for them to say no during face-to-face meetings—something they could easily do via email.

It was also helpful to read their body language during those meetings which helped me understand if the response was honest or if they were trying to placate me just to move me along. It's impossible to see body language through email.

At other times the person appeared so uncomfortable that I decided to back off from the request because of their in person reaction. It's likely that some heartache was saved by taking that action.

Face to face delivery of messages and important mission objectives became my primary method of communicating with the teams I led. It was very easy to motivate them in person by a show of the passion I had for the particular project or mission. Reading the pulse of the group was also much easier in person than through a constant exchange of emails.

Face-to-face leadership became my mantra with other leaders as I traveled and served around the world. A simple call to a colleague would start with the phrase, "Come on by and have a cup of my coffee." They knew we needed to talk and that something of importance was on the table.

In later years military assignments took me to many foreign countries, mostly in the Middle East. In this region, we found that leaders of nations and leaders of military units all practiced this leadership lesson that I had learned years before.

No matter who you were, no matter how important your position was, there was going to be some respect shown between two people before anyone got down to business in that part of the world. There would be a cup of coffee, tea, or some local fruit juice served in a fancy glass. Regardless of the substance, that show of respect had to take place first before any business took place.

Those who failed to show this level of respect often found doing business in that part of the world very difficult. Fortunately for me, I learned this lesson early on and did not make mistakes at the international level. We drank many cups of coffee, tea and glasses of juice, but we represented the Air Force well and got a bunch of work done, thereby improving security around the world.

It's time to get on board. Get out of your office the next time you need something done or you need to add someone to your team or project. Go see them face-to-face and have a **c*up of their coffee***.

7

A GOOD MIRROR

Driving through an entry control point leading into the aircraft parking area on yet another extremely hot desert day in Iraq, the general and I would soon be escorting the Secretary of the Air Force and several high level dignitaries. During the dry run for this tour, I noticed an Airman standing post who appeared to have a full face beard. No problem right? Except that facial hair while in an Air Force uniform is strictly forbidden unless specifically waived for medical reasons.

Even when someone was granted a waiver to have full facial hair, it had to be trimmed neatly, and maintained within length standards. This particular Airman stood out because his beard appeared to be thick and it was extremely dark black hair. And in my opinion, an Airman who had a waiver from the standards, meaning he did not meet the standards, was not the person I wanted representing this high speed combat wing in front of the senior Air Force leader during his visit.

As the senior enlisted leader present it was my responsibility to ensure that all standards were being met and that we presented a good solid image at all times. Shortly after passing through, I notified his manager that I would like him switched out from that post before the Secretary came through. I moved on and never thought about it again.

Hours after the official dignitary visit was over, the manager who I contacted earlier decided to send me an email with his thoughts on my decision from earlier. Reading his email with close scrutiny was essential to ensure my understanding of the purpose of his email. What immediately jumped off the page were the sentences typed in all capital letters. Then the highlighted text stood out. Finally, the underlined and bold typed words jumped at me, all of which appeared to have been done to express his passion for the message he was trying to present.

After reading it to the end the first time I sat back in my chair and took a deep breath. This email certainly required a second read to see if it gave the same impression before taking any action or responding in any way.

The second read made the situation worse. During this second review, the language he used came through clearer than it did on the first read. That was likely caused by the focus on the highlights and non-standard text. It finally hit me during this second read that he was yelling at me with his typing in an effort to argue the point made earlier about his Airman who was not meeting standards for dress and appearance.

A quick glance to the top of the page really grabbed my attention as it showed that not only was he yelling at me through this electronic format, but he had copied several of his, and my, subordinates on this message. Not only was he yelling at me on email, he was doing so with his subordinates standing by and taking notice.

After some time and careful thought, my reply on email

looked like this: "...call my office." My reply went to all recipients, just as he had included originally, just so they knew this situation was going to be addressed. When the manager called me, he was immediately invited over for some much needed feedback.

When he arrived in my office he was invited in cordially. After brief pleasantries, I informed him that I intended to provide him with some direct feedback about the situation earlier in the day, and most specifically about the way he approached it. It went like this:

"I am going to give you some feedback about your handling of the situation today involving the Secretary and the method you used to convey your response. During this feedback I'd ask that you not respond to my inputs. I'd prefer you just listen. Feel free to write any notes you would like." He looked at me and said, "You mean you don't want me to ask questions or say anything?"

"That's correct, just listen and take notes, not responding immediately to what I say, or defending your actions. When we are complete there is only one thing I want to hear from you and that is, thank you. After that you can depart and do what you want with my feedback. This is not personal, its business and it's intended to improve your performance." He acknowledged and we moved on.

Sitting forward in his chair, he looked intently with pen and paper ready. "It's apparent that you do not agree with my direction from earlier today during the Secretary's visit. While I respect your desire to debate the issue, I do not appreciate the method with which you tried to convey that debate."

At this time he tried to interrupt and explain himself. I interrupted him, reminding him that he was not to speak, just take notes and listen. Reluctantly he sat back, gritting his teeth. I continued; "By choosing to send me an email rather than call me or see me in person I did not have the benefit of seeing your passion through non-verbal communication. I was left to interpret the tone of your message on my own. I've read each line of the email more than once to ensure that I truly understood your position. However, while reading it was hard to overlook the bold type, underlines, italics, highlights and capitalized words. Frankly, this came across as you yelling at me through your email."

Again he tried to interject and I motioned to him that I was not finished, and he was not to speak. He sat back and I noticed a change in his emotions, but I continued anyway. I looked back at him and continued with the conversation.

"Your email appeared to be an attack on my decision making. It appeared to be directly combative toward a lawful request that was made for the betterment of the entire unit under the circumstances. And it appeared to be an attack on me, all under the watchful eyes of the subordinates you copied on the email."

At that moment there was a silence in the room that needed no explanation. After a short pause I continued the conversation; "The action you took today in response to the situation was not proper and will not be tolerated in this unit. In the future, when you have something you would like to debate with me, take the time to contact me in person so that we can have the full discussion, face to face. I will listen to your thoughts and consider your request or actions. But I will not tolerate the method you used to convey your message on this occasion. If you cannot get to me personally, you need to reach me by phone and at least give me the benefit of hearing your voice."

He tried hard to hold back, but could not contain himself, he needed to speak. Before he could get words out, I finished my thoughts; "At this time I would just like you to say thanks and depart. That way you can have time to consider the feedback I have given you and if there is a need for more discussion, we can sit down together later and make that happen."

He stood and began to depart my office. As he got to the door he turned and cleared his throat. Looking back at me, he said: "Thank you, that is the first time in my entire career, in fact my entire life, that anyone has given me real direct and honest feedback. Thank you." He turned and left the office.

Later that week the manager was seen moving about the combat unit displaying a whole new attitude. He was walking taller and moving with a purpose. He approached me and again thanked me again for the feedback. Throughout the next six months we worked together closely and never again had problems communicating because I took the time to give him this direct feedback.

This feedback made him look into the mirror and see how his actions were impacting others. I was a good mirror for him, one that reflected his actions and made him consider what he had done. This reflection made him change some behaviors that contributed to an improved leadership standard for him as he led men and women in combat.

On this particular occasion, I was A ***Good Mirror*** for someone who never had one before.

THE LESSON

Find a Good Mirror that provides you with honest feedback and does not hide your flaws

- *Keep that mirror close and look to it often for feedback*

- *Avoid getting feedback from every mirror you see*

THOUGHTS FOR SUCCESS:

During a formal training course on giving and receiving feedback I learned the importance of keeping feedback a professional matter and never allowing it to become personal. That training really paid off in this case, giving me the upper hand to handle the situation properly.

Had I taken this manager's actions as a personal attack on me, I may have responded in a harsh manner, creating even more of a battle and missing the chance to resolve the issue. He may not have learned from his mistake on the proper way to address another leader.

As you can see from the story, we never even debated the direction that I gave him that day, we focused on his actions and the impact it had on the mission. To some readers, the approach I used in providing this feedback may have seemed too harsh because some leaders don't like to be direct and to the point, and often don't like to enter into a possible controversial situation with subordinates.

I've learned that giving feedback in this manner allows you to remain professional and non controversial. It's a safe way to offer feedback and leads toward positive change in behavior.

Leaders are fortunate that they normally have enough self-esteem and confidence so that they can operate alone or without much support. Leadership can also be a lonely venture placing you in situations where you have to stand your ground alone and without the support of those on your team. When this happens, you will want and need some feedback from a mirror that can provide you with good information about your performance and decisions.

Often this mirror will be someone outside of your organization. It may be a personal mentor you have identified with in the past. Your mentor or mirror can provide you with sound advice on how to navigate through tough times as a leader. The key is to always seek honest and direct feedback from a reliable source.

Unfortunately, if you find yourself operating without ever getting any feedback on your actions, failure may be right around the corner. You can lull yourself into believing that everything is going well when it really is not.

Remember that A Good Mirror:
- Won't hide your flaws because they are worried about hurting your feelings
- Will provide tough feedback when it would be easier to reflect on just the good
- Will tell you the whole truth, even when it stings

There are also bad mirrors that:
- Only tell you good things that you do, leaving out what you really need to hear
- Come with personal objectives for their own gain

Don't become so consumed with mirrors that you never pass by one. Some leaders seek feedback from everyone they encounter. People who seek that much feedback are normally insecure and need reassurance. Unfortunately if you are seeking feedback from many sources, they won't have much to offer that has real value. Just find a Good Mirror and stick with that one.

This same lesson can be applied to your personal life, just as it can in business. Just be sure to never confuse the two. Feedback on your professional actions should never become a personal matter. You should clearly separate personal and professional matters. However, in your personal life you can also find a mirror that can keep you grounded in your actions and help you get back on track when you stray.

It can start with family and the upbringing that you had. In my family we were taught honesty and integrity, so looking for feedback was easy for me...most times I did not even have to ask. This beginning translated well into my professional life and I found it easy to trust those in my inner circle to tell me when things were not going well or when I needed to make an adjustment.

At home, my wife provided that feedback to me across the many years in all aspects of life. She is always willing to give direct and honest feedback on matters that are important, and she never holds back on what is needed to be heard. You need A Good Mirror in your personal life as well.

Go find **A Good Mirror** and keep them close. Be **A Good Mirror** for those in need!

8
IMPROVE THE FOXHOLE

I remember vividly hearing the acceptance speech made by the late Jimmy Valvano, former coach of the national champion North Carolina State Wolfpack men's basketball team in 1993 upon receiving the Arthur Ashe Courage Award. His speech included a statement about knowing where you had been, knowing where you are, and knowing where you are going.

Those words became something very important to me as my professional career progressed. Although he was dying from an inoperable brain tumor, Coach Valvano saw clearly how important these things were to each of us. He went on to talk about having enthusiasm for life...another thing I have found important in my progress. Being enthusiastic around other people created a positive atmosphere that helped overcome many obstacles.

Following the terrorist attacks on America in September 2001, many of us in the military found ourselves in search of answers to many of life's bigger questions. As I wondered what the future held for me, I quickly found myself starting a long run of combat deployments that would help me find many of those answers in the professional realm.

This string of deployments would provide leadership challenges far beyond what was ever expected, so the lessons piled up quickly. The bottom line; I needed to find ways to motivate people toward some tough goals and objectives that were laid in front of us.

Leading into a deployment it was easy to have a plan, a set of ideas that should easily work, and plenty of enthusiasm to make it all happen. No challenge too tough. It was my time to make a difference in combat for my nation.

We hit the ground running with dogged determination and dug in fast to figure out what needed to be done. Quickly, we realized that our location lacked certain things that were within our capability and we got to work putting them in place.

It all seemed natural for me, but to some, it came across as "re-inventing the wheel." Why not leave it the way we found it some would say. Why are we working so hard to improve when we know the next team behind us will just change everything once we are gone?

Late one hot afternoon, as we were laying a line of concertina wire out on the open desert floor it became clear to me that what we were doing was improving our foxhole. We had to improve it in order to keep the enemy out and allow us to accomplish the task of flying combat missions. We had to protect our flanks and all avenues of approach.

We contemplated why the team deployed before us had not done this, but I reminded the team that they had a different set of challenges and we should not focus on what they did not do, but rather on what we needed to do.

As our deployment began, the base itself was growing in size and population, and the additional traffic would increase the possibility that enemy forces could approach and breach the perimeter. There was no time for relaxation or complacency during this tour of duty.

As the line was being laid, one of the guys asked why we were working so hard to improve things when the team before us had not. I told him that it was important for us to make these improvements now because things change with time and circumstances.

He looked at me with a look of confusion so I reminded him again that we don't know what it was like for them in their time or what other priorities they had to deal with. I told him that it's quite possible they wanted to lay this perimeter line out but never got to it because they were building up the tent city that we enjoy each night once our mission is complete. This explanation seemed to make sense and he and the others went back to work in the scorching sun.

I thought long and hard about the theory and how I could ingrain it in myself, and then share it with others to make it all worthwhile.

As a fan of military history I knew that in World War II American troops spent days on end sitting in Foxholes along some front line of the battlefield.

By today's standards we call those same locations, Defensive Fighting Positions, but everyone understood the term Foxhole, so I decided to incorporate that into the first lesson of this deployment.

The phrase ***Improve the Foxhole*** became our mantra. We decided that we would work hard each day to make our location better for the next team or at the very least, leave it better than we found it. My teams were taught that no matter what we found or what the conditions were when we started a new mission, we would not complain. It was clear that we did not have the same set of circumstances that our predecessors had and therefore we should not spend time worrying about it. We definitely did not need to take time to complain about it.

Occasionally, people became frustrated and made comments about other deployment teams. They felt like the people before them didn't get anything done. When those were heard, I would immediately stop them in their tracks and remind them that we did not have their circumstances. We did not have the same weather conditions or even the same threat from the enemy. Since we were not here with them, we should be slow to criticize them and just move on with what we have in front of us. I would always end the conversation with, "Let's just improve the foxhole and move on."

A year after that first deployment, my team was sent to Baghdad International Airport to maintain security of the most dangerous airport in the world. Each night brought on a series of attacks from enemy ground weapons, rockets and mortars. Rarely a night went by without a barrage of outgoing artillery from our brothers and sisters in the United States Army Artillery units placed around the perimeter.

Every night there were wounded warriors brought into the hospital for critical medical care. This mission would possibly be the toughest one we would ever face. It would have been easy to sit back and accept the status quo, not making any changes because we needed our rest by day, preparing for the attacks of the evening.

Instead, working 20 hours a day became the norm. The enemy always seemed to stop attacking between 2am and the late afternoon, so this was our time to handle improvements. A team of physical security specialists was scheduled for daily repairs to the fence line and entry points. It was the safest time for them to operate heavy machinery and the least likely time for the enemy to attack.

We produced a running log of the things that needed our attention for immediate improvement. Most of the work consisted of placing barriers, wires and obstacles to secure the perimeter. They were the hardest working bunch of warriors you have ever seen. They had learned from our previous combat deployment that by Improving the Foxhole was critical to mission success.

On many occasions they were asked by the forces standing watch on the perimeter why they worked so hard and changed so much stuff each day. I smiled each time I heard the question because the answer would always be the same. "We're here to improve the foxhole" one of them would proudly state. It nearly brought tears to my eyes that the lesson was so ingrained at this point that I didn't need to say it.

The completion of our mission in Baghdad happened as the capture of Sadaam Hussein shocked the world. Knowing that we had a direct hand in preparing the place where he would be held following his capture gave us reason for great pride in our work.

As we moved on to the next mission, another location inside of Iraq, we knew there was only one thing we could do, *Improve the Foxhole!*

The Lesson

Improve the foxhole by leaving things better than you found them through innovation and challenging the status quo

-    *Setting this tone will improve the chance of success for the next person and the entire organization*

THOUGHTS FOR SUCCESS:

Everyone has had the chance to come into a new place, a new job, or a new opportunity. When you got there you were faced with several choices. First and easiest on the list would have been to sit back and take it all in, accepting the status quo. You could have cruised through the assignment or set your feet in concrete for the long haul.

I believe the Improve the Foxhole lesson can be applied to the business culture today. Any time you take over a new job, or a new position as a leader of a team, there will be opportunities for improvement.

If you go in as the new boss and accept the status quo during your time, the team and ultimately the organization may fail to improve. However, if you encourage improvement on a continuous basis, making it better for the next person, you will likely be viewed as a progressive leader who cares about the team and the organization.

In some sectors of the business world this is known as Innovation. Employees are encouraged to come up with innovative ideas and submit them to their leaders for consideration. Working together with employees, leaders can help improve the organization by encouraging this type of behavior.

You may find yourself with easier circumstances than those presented in combat, but the challenge for the leader remains the same. Accept the status quo and possibly miss opportunities for improvement. Or **Improve the Foxhole** in order to make the team better and contribute more to the overall organization.

As a leader, I was once thrust into a situation where previous managers had tried to accomplish their mission by accepting the status quo. They made little progress, and the team was more in control of daily operations than management was. Something had obviously not been working as the team was in disarray. Morale was low, teamwork was non-existent, and most employees found themselves not wanting to come to work. Something had to change, this foxhole needed huge improvement...and fast.

An important point for leaders in this situation is to know what can be changed and when to change it. For instance, there are some things that can be changed right away. In this particular scenario, the employees required a high level of discipline to complete the mission. However, I found that discipline was lacking and it all started with a lack of concentration on the fundamentals of the job. The first and most important thing that needed to change was the basic discipline and accountability of the individuals. Understanding that one could not wait or the same problems would persist, the team would remain in a hole, and I would fail as a leader.

Change is never easy for people to accept and being a new leader does not give you instant credibility with employees to make sweeping changes. Therefore, it's smart to work on the critical ones first and try to understand and evaluate all the others you know are less critical to mission success.

Helping employees understand the need for change can be hard. I found this theory effective in helping those stubborn employees get over the fear of change and move forward with the organization.

I told them we would build a wall between the past and the present. Then, I promised that I would become the foundation on the current side of the wall, allowing them to be more successful as they operated in the present.

All they had to do was accept that going back over the wall and performing like they had previously was no longer acceptable. That once they all operated on the right side of the wall, we could move forward and become more successful.

In cases like this one, the individual employees needed to improve their own personal foxholes before they could actively participate in helping the team. Once that transition took place, the overall performance of the team improved and the mission was the beneficiary.

The next time you find yourself moving into a new position, or taking over new responsibility, make an early assessment about how you can *Improve the Foxhole*.

9

THE LEADERSHIP LINE

This day started like most other in the combat zone, an early rise followed by a quick breakfast in a loud and crowded dining facility. This dining facility, like most in the combat zones was constantly packed with troops coming from and going on tough missions, meaning they were always hungry and always spirited. There is no such thing as a quiet meal in a combat dining facility.

Following a quick meal, we headed out for a one hour drive along the most dangerous stretch of highway in Central Asia. Speeds were not controlled by any local authority. Drivers lacked the proper driving skills for the speeds they traveled at, so there were often fatal accidents along this route. I remember having felt much safer traveling the streets of Baghdad years earlier...and this was in a civilized, allied country. Fortunately the travel was uneventful, just as we had hoped the rest of the day would be.

The plan called for meetings with deployed forces, to share a few of the latest leadership messages, and answer questions about what was going on. Before long the day would be done and I would be moving on for more of the same at another base.

Shortly after arrival at the location, an international airport with a military passenger terminal and a huge cargo operation, I detected many signs of stress among the team. The senior person on scene said that everything was OK, but I was still not convinced, there was just something in the air.

As we headed for the large gathering area where I would speak to a crowd of 200 I noticed a member of my unit standing off to the side in the waiting area. Thinking this was strange, I walked over and spoke to him, asking if he was OK. He showed obvious signs of stress, but he also said he was OK, and that he would be traveling soon. Although I could not put my finger on it, there was definitely something everyone else knew but me.

As we walked into the gathering, I was asked if it would be OK for us to take a break if we got notice of the honor cordon that would need to be formed. (An honor cordon was formed during the dignified transfer of a fallen warrior by all available Airmen. They formed two lines, facing each other, and standing shoulder to shoulder from the ramp of the plane as far as they could go. The Fallen would move through the cordon on their way to the aircraft for their final flight home, known as the Angel Flight.) Of course I agreed, and then asked who the honor cordon was for.

Suddenly there was clarity to the situation previously encountered. The intelligence report had arrived late the previous evening that an Explosive Ordnance Disposal (EOD) specialist had been killed in Afghanistan. I was unaware of the plans for his transportation home, and had not put it together myself before now.

It became clear to me that our honor cordon, the stress I was detecting, and the member of my unit standing by for transport was all because the fallen Airman from Afghanistan. I instructed the team that we would stop and perform the honor cordon no matter what, and that it would be my highest honor to join them.

Sometime later the room was interrupted by the call for an honor cordon. The room emptied immediately and more than 100 service members marched in formation to the waiting aircraft.

Once there, they formed two lines, facing inward and remaining silent. As the white transport vehicle approached carrying the fallen warrior, a booming voice sounded, "Detail, Attention!" In unison the formation snapped to attention. That was followed by "Present, Arms." Again, like a well oiled machine, more than100 right arms rose slowly to render honors.

As the flag covered casket passed, tears rolled down many of the faces...faces of those who never knew the man inside. Minutes later a chaplain administered a final prayer with a group of ten of us standing nearby, including the escort official—the member of my unit I had encountered earlier. Solemnly, we all rendered a final salute and wished our warrior and his escort Godspeed and a safe journey home on the Angel Flight.

We reformed the group back in the room and completed the discussion we had previously started. Once complete, we headed back to the passenger terminal, where much to our surprise, stood the fallen warrior's escort. Within seconds we learned that he had been removed from the plane because of a technicality with his paperwork and that he was told he was not authorized to accompany the fallen warrior home. He was devastated...I was furious.

He desperately wanted to be on that plane and be the first one to meet the family on arrival. My immediate thought was that this situation was completely unacceptable and nowhere near normal. However, situations like this do not always go the way they are planned and sometimes there are deviations…this deviation needed to be dealt with fast.

There was no clear black and white rules set to govern this type of movement, and common sense did not always apply. I knew immediately that something had to be done, so we jumped into action.

Within a few seconds, I approached the civilian in charge of the airfield and demanded the plane to stop where it was and give us a minute to figure out what went wrong with the paperwork. Phone calls were made to the headquarters that controlled all air movement for the Central Command area of operations.

At one point, I was talking with the control center by phone, the civilian running the passenger terminal, the Army Sergeant who controlled paperwork, and several people who were with me at the time.

As things were being worked out, I directed someone to take the fallen warrior's escort in a vehicle and drive out to the location of the aircraft and to "…park in front of it if you have to." As I gave this direction, we were notified that the aircraft was already on the runway, cleared for takeoff. I was not done, and had to continue this effort to get him back on that plane.

Completing the phone call to the headquarters I slammed the phone down and instructed the civilian to direct the plane back to the parking spot and to take on this passenger. Reluctantly, he took my direction and requested the plane to return and park. He told me that he was not happy about it and that this would probably come back to haunt me.

At that moment, I was willing to accept whatever punishment came my way, because what I was doing was absolutely the right thing to do.

About that time, the U.S. Army Sergeant who was responsible for this program returned to the passenger terminal and said that his team had made a mistake and the escort was actually authorized to be on that plane. I threw the paperwork down on the counter for the civilian and headed out of the terminal without saying a word.

Arriving at the aircraft parking spot a few minutes later, I told the escort that things were worked out and that he was getting back on that plane and taking his battle buddy home to his family.

There was not much need for more words. As he started to board the plane he simply turned and grabbed me in a battle hug. He looked me in the eye and said thanks, then walked onto the stairs of the plane. At the top of the stairs he turned and waved, and I believe I could see a sense of relief on his face, as he was going to be able to fulfill the highest duty a combat warrior can complete.

Weeks after this experience took place, the escort official shared an email story with the entire EOD community. He shared with them that his journey was nothing like the one portrayed in the movies. His was filled with obstacles, but they were all overcome by leaders who cared and knew how to get things done by going outside the line.

The Lesson

Work in the grey areas on those situations that don't fit neatly on the leadership line

- *Sometimes a leader has to make a decision based on other factors that fall outside of the line...in the grey areas left and right of the line*

- *A leader has to be willing to stand up to the decisions they made and accept any consequences that may come their way*

THOUGHTS FOR SUCCESS:

The circumstances in this case were not close to the standard line. Had we stuck to the standard line and not looked to the grey areas, this escort would have been left behind at that airport and our warrior would have gone home alone. He deserved better.

Any leader can operate from a position of always staying on the leadership line, or working strictly in the black and white. This is a safe and easy position to take. These leaders know the rules and stick to them, never considering what falls to the left (normal exceptions to policy) and to the right (unusual exceptions to the policy).

For those leaders who stick to the leadership line and never venture into the grey areas left and right, tough decisions will rarely, if ever, be made. They will push that decision off to the dismay of their followers. I learned this theory during a pre-deployment training course from a trusted leader who always made us think outside the line. His wisdom and knowledge took us out of our comfort zone and directly impacted our ability to operate in the grey areas.

Leaders who are comfortable working in the grey areas left and right are often seen as problem solvers by their followers. They find solutions when others cannot. They consider all known factors, including the written rules, and then make decisions based on every known piece of information, including the potential cost of making a decision that does not fit neatly on the line.

In order to teach this lesson to new leaders I use this simple exercise:

- Start by drawing a line on a sheet of paper.

- Make it go vertical from top to bottom and in the middle of the page
- Place two X's out to the left of the line
- Place two X's out to the right of the line

To explain the drawing, I tell them that the line in the middle represents the written rules or the standards. It can be policies, rules, guidelines, or any other form of information that relates to your organization's governing principles.

The X's on the left represent the situations that are abnormal, but reasonable and known (normal exceptions to policy). They have been seen before, dealt with, and we know the usual outcome.

The X's on the right side represent those unusual situations that we have not experienced, and don't always know what the outcome will be (unusual exceptions to the policy).

In the story above, I was working on the extreme right side, dealing with the unusual situation where there was nothing normal to consider. I had to make the decision to demand that aircraft return even though I knew I could be held personally accountable for any backlash that came from making them divert from their flight plans or passenger manifest.

I considered everything and then made the decision based on what was the right thing to do. In the end, I would have easily have been exonerated because he was authorized on that plane...we just did not know it when I made the decision. It takes understanding, knowledge, experience, and courage to make decisions outside of the leadership line.

Leaders who work only on the line rarely take risks and often frustrate their people. Leaders who work the left X's are often successful, but not seen as risk taking. Certainly they remain a little risk averse, which can be interpreted as being weak, or not willing to make a tough decision.

Leaders who can work the X's on the right are seen as risk takers. Those who take risks that are somewhat calculated and based on knowledge remain very successful. Those who jump into the right side X's without fully understanding the consequences may find themselves in hot water from time to time. But given the situation, the consequences may validate the risk.

As a leader it became easy to earn a reputation for operating outside the leadership line successfully. Throughout many years of leadership responsibility it became easier to operate in those grey areas and I cannot remember a time when I regretted being there.

If I had remained a black and white leader my entire working life, I am certain that I would have missed out on many memorable experiences like the one on that airport where I made it possible to send a fallen warrior home with his escort.

I'm glad that I took those chances and worked the grey areas around the **Leadership line**.

10
COURAGEOUS LEADERSHIP

The weather was unusually warm on that October afternoon in 2006 on the mean streets of Baghdad, Iraq. Regardless of the conditions, a group of Security Forces Airmen went headlong into their mission of training Iraqi Police across the Karadah District of Baghdad.

A team of 13 Airmen, each with a specific role to play in the proper execution of the day's mission was quietly forming in the compound. Nobody knew what circumstances were in front of them or the tragedy that awaited them.

For one young Security Force Airman, it would be his last mission. He was assigned as the heavy machine gunner, posted in the turret of a heavily armored humvee—known as the most vulnerable position because of the exposure it created for the person.

This particular Airman often volunteered for this role as he did not like having his friends and co-workers exposed to the extra danger. Today's challenge included supporting the Iraqi Police after locals found an Improvised Explosive Device (IED) on the streets. The team responded to handle the situation just as they had many times before.

Immediately after arriving on scene, the brave young man rose from the turret of his vehicle in an attempt to stop women and children from entering the area. Within the first minute after arrival, he was shot and killed instantly when a sniper's bullet struck.

The team had no idea they were set up for this attack, and now the only thing the team could do was escape and evade the attack zone and hope to reach medical care in time to save their teammate.

Sadly, before they could make much progress at all, the team leader came to the realization that he had lost one of his men. A helicopter arrived and rapidly flew this injured warrior away to the combat surgical hospital, but it was too late. The team was in shock as they headed back to the camp. This was a tragic day for the team, the entire unit, and all of us in Iraq at the time.

One of the toughest duties a military leader is tasked with is facing tragedy in situations like this. A colonel with nearly 30 years in the Air Force and his senior enlisted advisor, a chief master sergeant, sped toward Baghdad to be with the unit as they dealt with the tragedy of the day.

With the honor cordon formed and the dignified transfer ceremony complete, this Fallen Airmen departed for the trip home on his Angel Flight. The other members of his unit returned to their compound and contemplated the long day and all that had taken place.

They sat around with long faces, covered in tears. The emotions they held in all day were now letting go. As the night lingered on, the colonel and his chief went around person to person checking to see if everyone was alright. Along this path, they came across a young man who seemed to be taking the tragedy extremely hard. He looked at the colonel and simply asked; "What do we do now, what's next?"

At that moment in time, the colonel found himself at a fork in the leadership journey we refer to as a "Courageous Leadership" moment. He had two choices on how to handle this situation, each with their own set of outcomes.

Without hesitation, the steely eyed colonel looked that young man in the eye and said; "I'll tell you what now. Tonight we sit together and mourn the loss of our friend and fellow Airman. We laugh, we cry, we think about all the good times and bad.

But what's next is tomorrow. For tomorrow we will mount up this team and go back out on the mission in the same streets of Baghdad." He paused for a few seconds and then said, "Because if it was worth our teammate giving his life for today, it's worth you and me doing it again tomorrow. So in his honor, we will go back out on the mission and complete it to the best of our ability."

The young Airman stood tall and thanked the colonel. He said, "Sir, thanks, that is exactly what I needed to hear."

The Lesson

Demonstrate courageous leadership by making the tough decisions during difficult times

- *Develop the ability to exercise **Courageous Leadership** by saying the right thing, making sure the right thing is done*

- *Continue encouraging people to stay focused on the task at hand*

THOUGHTS FOR SUCCESS:

Imagine for a minute what would have happened if he had chosen differently. Let's go back to that moment and have the colonel say something like, "I'm not sure what now. I'm worried that we did not have the right equipment or procedures in place." Or he may have said that he was not sure we had the right training for the mission we were on.

Imagine if he had said, "Maybe it's too dangerous out there and we may need to keep you guys inside the wire and not send you out on those missions."

Had he chosen the other direction at the fork, the easy route, those Airmen would have lost all confidence and likely not finished the mission. But he chose to make the courageous decision and stand up to the strains of the moment, never losing faith in the training and capabilities of the team. His courage carried over to the rest of the Airmen on that team, and they went on to complete the remainder of their deployment without another incident.

Leadership is easy when placed in the right context. During combat operations the price of decisions made by leaders is significantly increased because of the consequences that come with failure.

In the private sector, the price of a leadership decision may very well be costly in a significant fashion. In business, the poor decision seldom leads to death and destruction of human life like it does in combat, but its impact on the business may be nearly as damaging.

For example, a leader in business may be faced with the tough decision to fire or terminate an employee because of poor performance. The employee may be well liked, may have a long standing tenure with the company and may even have had great success in the past.

But when faced with circumstances where the employee no longer performs in the manner the company needs or expects that employee needs to go.

For leaders in business this will require you to act with Courageous Leadership, just as the colonel did that day in Baghdad. No, the circumstances may not be as critical, but your courageous leadership will be needed.

You have to make the right choice for the company, even when you know you are going to cause financial hardship for an employee. At that time you have to separate yourself from the humanistic portion of leadership and make the decision based on what is good for the business. It will be tough, but you have to make the decision.

During the leadership journey you should expect to come to many crossroads. There will be opportunities where you are given multiple choices for making a decision. Each comes with its own impact on the people or the business at hand.

Some will provide easy paths for you as a leader, while others will take you into unknown territory.

If you ever find yourself faced with a life altering decision like the one from the compound in Baghdad that day, I am hopeful this lesson will help you through that difficult situation.

If you get to that fork in the leadership journey and choose to make the Courageous Leadership choice, you will gain the trust and respect of your people and they will follow you anywhere.

Leaders who choose the other route soon lose their people and the negative impact may be long lasting. Employees like leaders who can make decisions and stand behind them. They really appreciate those who can make the courageous leadership decision.

Get out there and be a **Courageous Leader**!

11

LOAVES AND FISHES

According to the Gospels, when Jesus heard that John The Baptist had been killed, he withdrew by boat privately to a solitary place.

The crowds followed Jesus on foot from the towns. When Jesus landed and saw a large crowd, he had compassion on them and healed their sick. As evening approached, the disciples came to him and said, "This is a remote place, and it's already getting late. Send the crowds away, so they can go to the villages and buy themselves some food." Jesus replied, "They do not need to go away. You give them something to eat." "We have here only five loaves of bread and two fish," they answered. "Bring them here to me," he said.

Jesus directed the people to sit down on the grass. Taking the five loaves and the two fish and looking up to heaven, he gave thanks and broke the loaves. Then he gave them to the disciples, and the disciples gave them to the people. They all ate and were satisfied, and the disciples picked up twelve basketfuls of broken pieces that were left over. The number of those who ate was about five thousand men, besides women and children.

This is one of the lessons from the Bible that I remember clearly from my childhood. Before becoming a leader of youth sports teams or even my time in the military, this lesson always got my attention. Maybe there was something special in this message that could be used as a leader.

The story of Loaves and Fishes appears in every version of the Gospel. Some may think it's a stretch to use this biblical story of a miracle as a leadership lesson, but trust me; it works...***Loaves and Fishes***.

Along the road to becoming a leader I found that it took a great deal of courage to take on challenges and help those who did not believe that things could get done during tough times. The decision to become a leader early in my career came with a commitment to two things; courage and belief.

Courage is explained in a previous chapter, so this lesson is more about faith and belief. Belief comes in many forms. You can have strong belief in the system you are currently in. You can also have belief in the people who work for you. Belief has few limitations. Quite simply, you are the one who limits how much you believe in your ability as a leader.

When you fully commit to having true belief in your ability to lead, you will find tough challenges become much easier. This theory worked well for me over the course of four combat tours where the challenges came in personal and professional lanes. My understanding of the importance in believing in my ability to lead grew with each new challenge. While I had a great understanding of this theory, I needed a way to share that with others so they could benefit as well.

I knew that I needed to be a strong leader with great confidence, one who could make decisions and stand behind them. I also knew that nobody wanted to work for a leader who lacked confidence and belief in their abilities--especially in combat situations.

January 2007: Sitting alone on the roof of the headquarters building one night in Iraq there was an overwhelming feeling that something special had to be done. We had just completed a memorial service for three American Airmen who were killed in action by the enemy's IED attached to a vehicle, and we were all hurting from the loss.

As the hours passed my pain grew deeper. This loss brought the total to seven Airmen killed in the line of duty in the first six months of this one year tour. The pain was magnified for me personally because just weeks before this horrible day I had visited these three Airmen in their camp where we laughed together and shared stories of our lives and the challenges of the battle ongoing in Iraq.

During that visit, I could not help but notice something was wrong with this team, but could not put my finger on it. As we departed their camp I asked the team leader if everything was OK, and he indicated it was. Somehow the feeling in my gut told me something different, but I departed without taking another action.

Back on the roof, I continued to ponder this overwhelming feeling that something needed to be done, and that we could not just memorialize these fallen warriors and move on as if nothing had happened. Maybe I could have done more for them during my recent visit. I kept asking myself that question and could not find a good answer. Either way, I had to do something tangible now that would help bring some solace to their sacrifice.

A light came on. Since there was nothing that could change their course of fate, there had to be something we could do to preserve their memory. We needed to finish building the Fallen Airman Memorial to create a place to honor them and all of the other Airmen who had been or would be killed in action during this fight in Iraq.

It would be a solemn place where their names could be placed on a wall as a lasting tribute to their sacrifice. It would also be a place where the rest of us could go to honor and remember them. Yes, the memorial had to be finished immediately.

The next morning a team of highly motivated members of the unit came together and set their minds to the memorial project. Time was of the essence, so we needed to move fast in order to finish the project before we completed our tour and headed for home. This was not a project that could be started and left for the next team to finish. A goal was set. We needed to finish the project and have it dedicated by Memorial Day 2007, the last week of May.

They looked at me like I was crazy, and rightfully so. Here we were in Iraq, busy with the daily execution of combat missions and all that it takes to care and feed a base of more than 10,000 people. How would we ever find the time and money to build and dedicate a monument in their memory? To many in the room the challenge seemed too tough. I knew of only one way to make this happen, we truly had to believe that we could do it.

Questions came from the team members. How much money do we have? What kind of materials can we get? Where will it go? Where will we get the name plates? And so many more. The questions were recorded and each item was discussed.

After assigning tasks to several of the members of the team, I urged them to go out and start working the different tasks they had been assigned and to leave the funding piece to me. Someone in the room looked at me and said, "Just where are you gonna get the money to build this memorial in that short of a time?" I looked around the room and took a collective breath, then said, "Loaves and Fishes!"

The group remained in the room long after my departure, talking among themselves. It would not be long before they appointed someone to come and find me for an explanation about my plan for the funding. He came into the office to discuss the matter with a worried look on his face. I told him, "Listen, I believe in this project strongly."

Although we only had a few dollars available from a special fund, I knew there would be enough money for this project. In fact I told him; "I believe that when we are done there will be enough left over for the long term maintenance needs of this memorial. Just like the story in the bible, Loaves and Fishes."

Stunned, he looked at me without saying much. From our experience together in another deployment, he knew that I was not a religious fanatic and he found it strange that a biblical story would be something used to lead a project of this magnitude. Looking him squarely in the eyes, I told him that I believe in this team and his ability to meet any challenge. I believe that if you all bring together your collective energy and effort that great things will happen and the memorial will be done in time.

And then I told him that I just believe, and sometimes believing is enough. I emphasized to him that our Fallen Airmen deserved to be honored in this way, so that we would never forget them. Together we decided to move out and get this effort started, building a place to properly honor our Fallen Airmen. As he departed, I could feel the growing belief in his spirit.

A very honorable ceremony was held at the Fallen Airman Memorial on that last weekend in May 2007. With more than 300 people in attendance, the memorial was unveiled on a dark cloudy day under an intense rain shower, a rare event in Iraq. That day 32 Airmen stood in formation as representatives of the Fallen Airmen from Operation Iraqi Freedom. This formation included the seven we had lost through January and two more we had lost since that day.

At the end of the ceremony, I walked into the office with the same person who challenged me at the first meeting. There was an envelope on my desk and he instructed me to pick it up.

Inside was a pile of money that had been donated and not needed to complete the project. In that envelope was several hundred dollars left over for maintenance and upkeep of the memorial by those who came to serve after our mission was complete.

I smiled like never before, and looked at him and said, **"Loaves and Fishes**."

The Lesson

Fully commit yourself to having belief that anything is possible with faith in your abilities to provide Loaves and Fishes

- Tough challenges become easier when you truly believe in yourself and your team

THOUGHTS FOR SUCCESS:

A year later, I found myself at the Air Forces Central Command Headquarters, located on Shaw Air Force Base in Sumter, South Carolina. Over the first few weeks of this tour, I made my way around the base taking in the people and places I would be responsible for.

It did not take long before the realization came to me that this Headquarters base should have a memorial itself, similar to the one in Iraq. But not only for those who died in combat while in Iraq, but to all United States Air Force Airmen who have been killed in action during all previous wars. Shortly after making this realization, a committee was formed and the challenge was levied.

During the first meeting of this new team, the same questions were brought out. Mostly, they worried about approval for placing a memorial on a military installation and about how it would be funded. Sitting back, I took in all of their questions and smiled. When they were complete, I simply said, *"Leave the funding piece to me...it's another case of loaves and fishes."*

Yes, they were stunned and wondered about the meaning of that comment. I explained that when it comes to doing something like building a memorial, something of value that was for a good cause, there will always be people willing to donate time, money, and resources. In fact, I assured them that we could raise enough funds to build the memorial and still have plenty left over for the future needs of the memorial.

At the first meeting we had no funds to start the project. Two years later, thanks to some generous people who believed in the honorable project, a beautiful memorial was dedicated on the side of a lake on Shaw Air Force Base. Not only was the memorial bigger and more detailed than originally designed, there was more than 10,000 dollars left over in the fund for future improvements and maintenance needs. At the end of the dedication ceremony someone from the committee came up to me and whispered, *"Loaves and Fishes...well done."*

The Loaves and Fishes lesson has been transferred from my battlefield experiences to the private sector office. It's proven that civilian employees feel the same way about following a leader who has a strong belief in them and their abilities. There is nothing to fear when true belief prevails...Loaves and Fishes.

While these two stories will not qualify as miracles and certainly don't rate the same attention as a biblical story they were taken from, they do help accentuate a point.

-   **If you believe in something strongly, and have the conviction to carry through with your beliefs, almost anything is possible**

Those two memorials stand today as my testament to believing in many things, including my own leadership capabilities. Ironically, as operations in Iraq came to a close in 2011, the original memorial from Balad Air Base in Iraq was not lost in the movement. Somehow that memorial found its way to Shaw AFB and sits on its own pedestal at the lake, right next to the memorial to all Fallen Airmen.

In the private sector, we face many challenges to make the business profitable. Using the lesson from Loaves and Fishes, showing a strong belief in your abilities and exuding that same level of confidence and belief in your employees, you will find few things you cannot overcome.

Believe in your own leadership. But don't think it will just come to you because you want to believe it will.

- Work hard, gain the trust of your people
- Select strong people and assign them tasks they are capable of completing
- Help them accomplish those tasks, building confidence in them

- Don't lose faith in your ability to lead the project or complete the mission
- You are the key to making your own story of *Loaves and Fishes!*

GLOSSARY OF THE LESSONS

THE MAILBOX STORY
Put Your Name on the Mailbox by showing pride in yourself and all that you own or control

STAY IN YOUR LANE
Stay in Your Lane by concentrating all of your effort and energy on the mission or task that you have been assigned

THE EQUIPMENT GUY
Spend time getting to know the Equipment Guy on your team or in your organization and ensure he knows how valuable he is to the team's success

JUST FIX TRUCKS
Make each employee understand how their task is important to the overall mission, even if they just fix trucks

WALK THE MILE
Earn the respect and trust of your
subordinates by Walking a Mile in their
shoes, experiencing what they go through
each and every day

A CUP OF MY COFFEE
Meet people face to face over a cup of
coffee to find out what you can do for each
other and how you can collaborate for
success

A GOOD MIRROR
Find a Good Mirror that provides you with
honest feedback and does not hide your
flaws

IMPROVE THE FOXHOLE
Improve the foxhole by leaving things
better than you found them through
innovation and challenging the status quo

THE LEADERSHIP LINE
Work in the grey areas on those situations that don't fit neatly on the leadership line

COURAGEOUS LEADERSHIP
Demonstrate courageous leadership by making the tough decisions during difficult times

LOAVES AND FISHES
Fully commit yourself to having belief that anything is possible with faith in your abilities to provide Loaves and Fishes

ABOUT THE AUTHOR

Scott H. Dearduff retired from the United States Air Force in January 2011 following more than 29 years of active duty service. At the culmination of his career he served as the Command Chief Master Sergeant for Ninth Air Force and United States Air Forces Central Command. He amassed more than 1000 days deployed to combat operations in the Central Command Area of Operations. Prior to his combat deployments in Iraq and Afghanistan, he served in more than 20 countries around the world and has traveled to more than 50 foreign countries worldwide. His leadership skills were honed under fire during nuclear security operations, Presidential security, disaster relief operations, humanitarian relief, aircraft accidents and an active shooter response with mass casualties. Along the way he obtained a Bachelor's Degree in Management and a double minor in Criminal Justice and Business Management. His military decorations include the Legion of Merit, 3 Bronze Star Medals, Afghanistan and Iraq Campaign Medals with multiple service stars, and the Air Force Combat Action Medal among more than 27 total decorations.

You may contact the Chief at dearduffconsulting@gmail.com or on the web site at www.dearduffconsulting.com

19351895R00056

Made in the USA
Charleston, SC
19 May 2013